Rooster's Balloon

A Child's Journey from Grief to Hope

written by Courtney P. Allen   illustrated by Patricia Calderon

Once there was a girl named Rooster. Well, her name was actually Mae, but everyone called her Rooster. When she was little, her parents always teased that she was their little rooster because she woke up so early in the morning.

Through the years, the name stuck. But her name wasn't the only thing unique about her; she also had a balloon. And not just any balloon. A balloon she took *everywhere*. She took it on walks. She took it in the car. She brought it to the grocery store. She even took it to the bathroom! Rooster loved her balloon very much.

Sometimes her balloon would get a little deflated so her daddy would have to blow extra air in it to puff it up. Rooster liked to make sure her balloon always looked its best.

Even though Rooster liked taking her balloon everywhere, there was one place that was extra special. It was a park with a beautiful garden. It had the sweetest smelling roses and the *loveliest* trees.

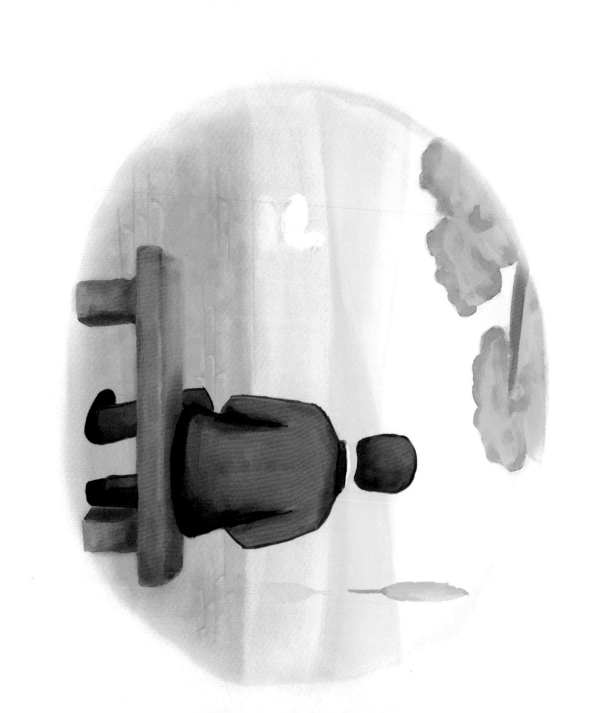

So she was extra excited when her mother told her they could go to her garden today. But on this day, when she got to the garden, she noticed a man sitting by a tree. Her tree. In her garden. Well, that's not nice, she thought. Doesn't he know this is my garden? Then she saw his face. He had a kind face. One that she recognized, but she couldn't remember how she knew him.

"Do *you* and your *balloon* want to come sit under the tree?" he asked, politely. Rooster knew she wasn't supposed to talk to strangers, but he had such a familiar face she thought it would be alright. Her mother told her it was ok so she walked over to him and sat down. Not too close though; he was still a stranger.

"Did you know this is my *garden*?" Rooster asked, in her sassy voice.

"No, I didn't know this was your garden. Do you want me to leave?"

"I mean, you can stay if you want. Why are *you* here?" Rooster couldn't help but ask.

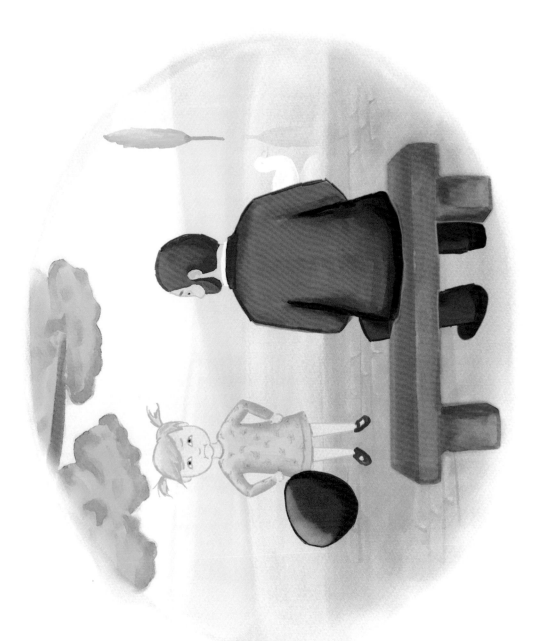

"I came to see *you*," he said.

*C*ame to see me? He doesn't even know me, she thought. She inched closer to him to get a better look. Those *eyes*. She knew those eyes.

"I know what you're *thinking*. You're thinking we don't know each other, but I've known you for a long time. I know your Mommy and Daddy, and I know all about your balloon," he said.

No way! This couldn't be true, Rooster thought. How could he know about my balloon? I've never told anyone the story of my balloon. "How could you know about my balloon if I've never told you about it?" asked Rooster.

"Do you mind if I tell you a *story* instead?" the man asked.

"OK," she said. She was glad they weren't talking about her balloon anymore.

"*Once* upon a time, there were two little girls, Mae and Grace, who were best friends. In fact, they were closer than best *friends*; they were sisters. They did everything together. They loved playing outside, putting on dress-up clothes, and getting into mischief of all kinds. They loved each other *very* much.

"One night their Mommy and Daddy put them to bed as they did every other night. They read a book, sang a song and said their prayers. They did the same thing *every* night. Hugs, kisses, and "I love yous" were given. The girls told each other "Night, night", and then they went off to sleep.

"The next morning, Mae woke up and realized Grace was gone. Not going to the potty gone, but gone like she's not coming back. She heard her parents say things like, "We didn't even know she was sick," and "It happened so fast." She saw her parents crying and lots of people started coming by to visit and bring food. Some of the food was good, some of it not so good. The people were really nice to her and tried to play with her, but they all had their sad faces on, so it wasn't very fun.

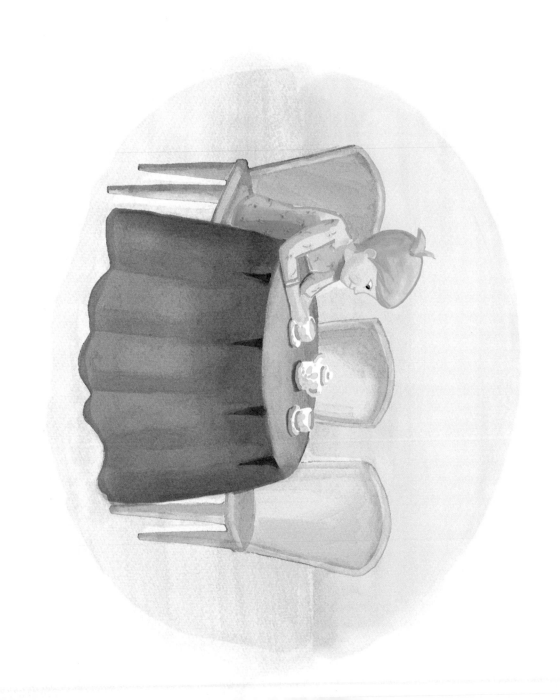

"Every day, Mae went from being sad to mad, then back to sad again. She wondered why Grace had left and why she stayed gone. Mae would even set a place for her at tea parties, hoping she'd come. But she never did.

"Then, one day, Mae found Grace's red balloon hiding in the back of the closet. It was the balloon they got the last time they went to the grocery store. She knew how much Grace had loved this *balloon*. So she decided she would carry it with her always in case her sister ever came back. Until then, the balloon could come to her tea parties and maybe the balloon could come to the park. The little girl took the balloon *everywhere* and..."

"Please stop," whispered Rooster.

"Don't you want to hear the rest of the story?" asked the man, gently. Rooster looked up at him with wide, tear-filled eyes. "How did you know?" she whimpered.

"Know what?" asked the man.

"That story. Who told you that story?" Rooster cried.

"No one told me. You see, I wrote that story," he said.

Rooster couldn't believe it. "But how could you have written that when it's MY story! It's about ME and MY Sissy!" she screamed.

"I know that too, child," he whispered.

"Well, did you know that I miss her everyday? Did you know that I didn't even know she was sick when she died? Did you know how much I loved her? All I wanted was to say goodbye."

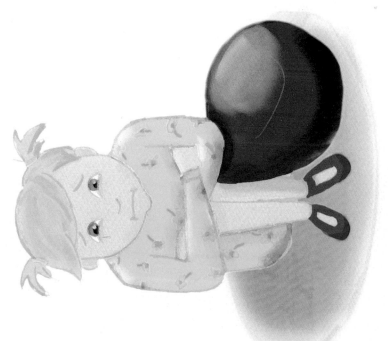

"Sweet Rooster, did you know that I love your sister very much? Did you also know that I have kept all the tears you've cried in a jar, and I carry them with me always?"

Rooster sat there and cried while the man put his arms around her. They were strong, but gentle, and made her feel safe.

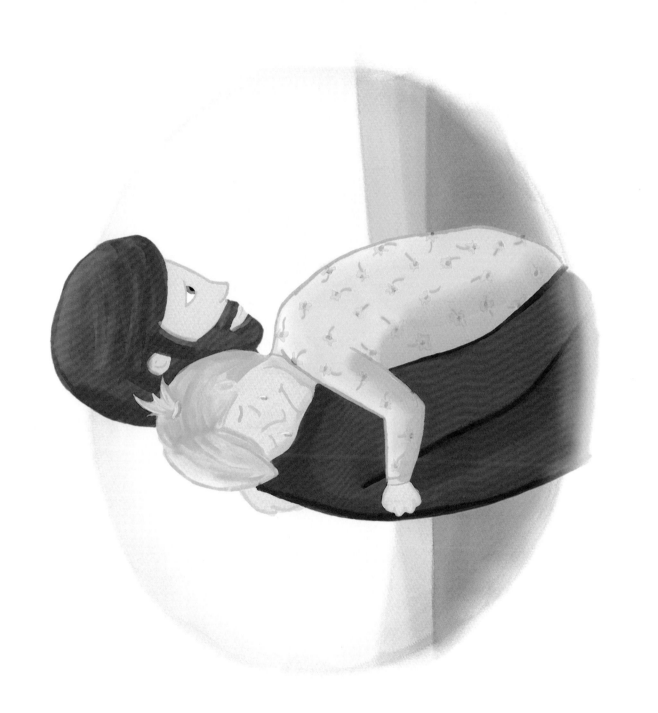

W hen Rooster was tired and had run out of tears, she asked, "So what happens next in my story?"

And, very *carefully*, the man answered, "You must let the balloon go."

Rooster sat up, scared. How could she just let the balloon go? She had worked so hard at taking care of it. She'd never lost it, not even once. If she let it go, there would be nothing left, and Sissy would be gone *forever*. No, absolutely not, she thought.

The man said, "I know this is not something you want to do. It will be very hard. But I will be with you. And instead of holding your balloon so tight, you can hold my hand. And if my hand is not enough, I'll pick you up and let you hug my neck as tight as you want and for as long as you need. I would do *anything* for you to know how much I love you. You may not always understand the things I let happen, just remember that I have a plan and it's good."

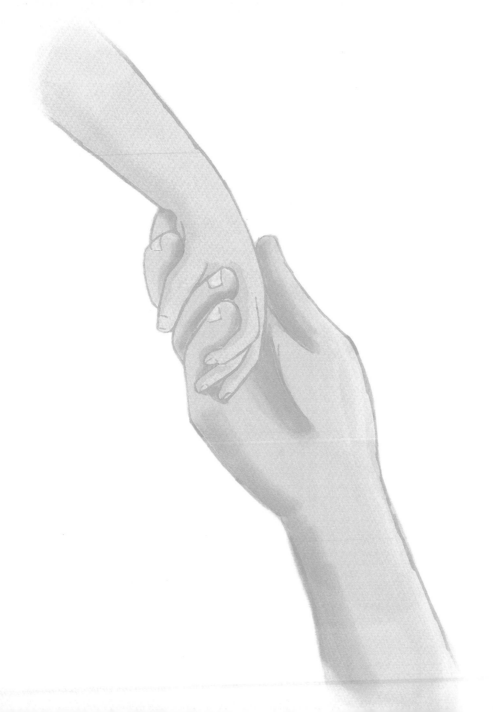

Rooster thought about what the man had said. She wasn't ready. Not yet. So she asked, "Do you think maybe we could take a walk, and you could hold my other hand a while?"

"Sure."

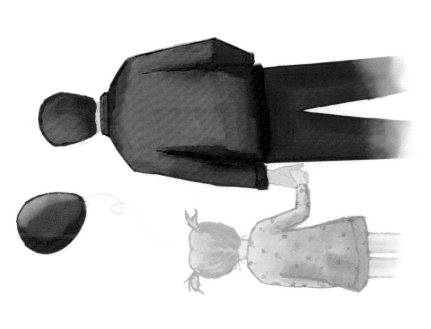

And as they walked, Rooster's grip on the string loosened. The more they talked, the safer she felt in the man's grip. Eventually, her fingers uncurled, and she let go of the balloon. As the balloon reached the clouds, Rooster could feel Sissy *reaching* into her heart. And Rooster knew that's where Sissy would stay.

*R*ooster still had a few questions for the man she needed answered. "Are you God?" she asked.

"I am," he said.

"Are you taking care of my Sissy?" she asked.

"I am," he answered.

"Where do the balloons go once you can't see them anymore?"

The man smiled. "To Heaven, of course."

Rooster *smiled*. Maybe Sissy will get to see her special balloon after all, she thought.

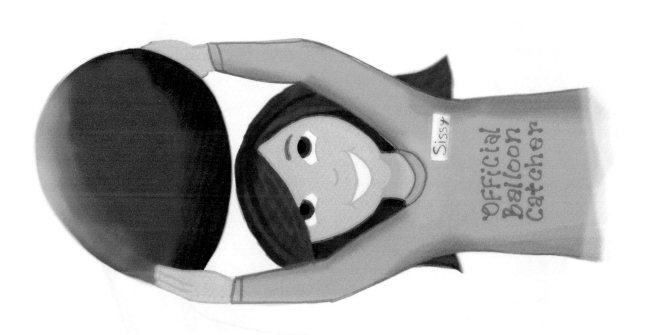

A portion of the proceeds from this book will
be donated to charity in honor of

Evie Grace Harrison.

Thank you for investing in the legacy of this sweet girl.

Copyright © 2015 PCB Press

PCB Press P.O. Box 2751 Brentwood, TN 37024
www.PCBpress.com

Printed in the United States of America by SelfPublishing.com

Library of Congress Catloging-In-Publication data:

Rooster's Balloon – 1st ed.
FIRST EDITION
p. cm.
ISBN 978-0-9970777-0-4

1. RELIGION 2. Christian Life 3. Death, Grief, Bereavement

10 9 8 7 6 5 4 3 2 1